# *Making Dollar$ and Cent$ Out of Online Dating*

By

Vivienne Diane Neal

**ISBN 13**: 9780615212753
**ISBN 10:** 0615212751

Dedicated to my mother who has been my biggest supporter, and who kept asking me, "When are you going to write a book."

I wish to thank all my customers, and members who have remained loyal throughout the years.

# *Table of Contents*

# Preface

Have you ever wondered what it is like to run an online dating site? Are you thinking about starting an online dating business, because you believe it is a source of income? Do you think you need a lot of money to get started? What is really in store for you if you do decide to take on this new venture?

Well be in awe no more. Vivienne Diane Neal, the founder of *One World Singles* and *One World Singles Blog*, takes a humorous and honest approach to explain the difficulties of starting and running an online dating Website on half a shoestring budget.

By no means is this a how to guide. This book is a personal journey into the ins and outs and the trials and tribulations she has faced in the past, trying to stay afloat in the ever-changing world of the Internet dating business.

If you are thinking about starting an online dating site or any type of online business, this book will give you a little insight as to what you <u>may</u> encounter.

*Making Dollar$ and Cent$*

*Out of Online Dating*

## *Chapter One*

## How It All Began

I have been in the dating business for over 20 years, and it has not been a cakewalk. In 1986, I started a pen pal club that over the years evolved into a worldwide correspondence and introduction service for singles and couples seeking friendship, romance, marriage and broadminded contacts. The service had members of all colors, ages (18+), ethnicities, religions, and lifestyles.

Contacts were made through a printed publication called *HMCS Romance International* and was sent through the US postal service (also known as snail mail) and featured descriptions, names and addresses along with photos of men and women from around the world.

The majority of my inquiries for pen pals came from outside of the USA, and most of my ads, on an exchange basis, were in foreign publications. Writing letters is very popular in many parts of the world. Soon, people began requesting introductions to men and women who were interested in more than just writing letters. People were interested in finding marriage minded partners and broadminded acquaintances. Therefore, I started to focus on the needs of my members. Business was good. This is not to say I was making a lot of money. I was not. My objectives were to provide optimum service and to maintain a loyal clientele.

Towards the end of the '90s, inquiries through the mail started to slow down. There were months when I did not make any money. Moreover, any money that I did make went right back into the business for advertising and marketing.

In October 2001, I decided to go on the Internet with my service to reach a broader market. The mission was the same, to target singles and couples. It was not an easy task. Of course, I knew it would take several years to build my site into an acceptable money making endeavor. Moving from mail order to the World Wide Web was like starting a new business.

I found a web-hosting service that provided several options to have a presence on the Internet. I started with a one-page design to introduce my service. My site provided contact information and an e-mail address for about two years. In the meantime, people were continuing to send inquiries through snail mail seeking information on my service. Some were interested in placing a personal ad on the Internet. At this point, it was time to expand my site to five pages. Then the hosting service decided to upgrade their site. Because of their new setup, I was having difficulties updating my site. At first, I thought it was my computer and my web browser causing the glitches, but this was not the case. After several weeks of trying to get support to find out what the problem was, there were no solutions. I decided to search for another web-hosting service that could meet my needs.

I found a service that provided all the tools needed to design my site. I purchased a ten-page web site builder and started to add links from other dating sites and affiliates. The photos and personal ads that appeared in my printed publication would now appear on the site. However, I discovered the hosting site did not have the capacity to publish all of the photos. Therefore, I had to search for a photo-hosting service.

Finally, I found one. The cost to use this service was very reasonable and within my budget. I was able to design the gallery, upload up to 1500 photos, along with personal profiles, and add the photo gallery to my dating Website. Therefore, anyone visiting the site would see the photos on my homepage. What was great about this particular photo hosting service was that I had the option of making my gallery public on their site. Anyone visiting the gallery would be able to click on the link to *HMCS Romance International.* Visitors could then obtain more information on our service and find out how to contact our members.

In February 2006, I decided to offer a more traditional online dating site for people who were not necessarily into the erotic scene. I searched for a dating network that could host my singles' site and still be able to maintain my own brand name. I found a company that already had a pre-installed database of over 100,000 profiles of singles. All I had to do was choose a domain name and register it, then advertise, and market my site to attract new members.

*One World Singles* was the name I gave my new dating site. My aim was to attract singles of all colors, ages (18+), religions, ethnicities and lifestyles to the site, which would provide the best online experience for singles worldwide. In addition, it was free.

I was prepared to give this site five years to grow into a successful money making service, just as I did with my correspondence club. Many specialists will tell you, it can take up to five or more years before a business begins to see a profit.

When you make a profit, you will be putting that money back into the business for maintenance, advertising, and marketing. I can attest to this. After all, I was not in this business to make a large bundle of money overnight and was prepared to provide a professional service and build my membership slowly. I wanted people who visited my site to know that I was going to be there for the long haul. The money will always follow.

After running *One World Singles* for one year, 456 people joined, and 1 percent became premium members. I thought this was good since *HMCS Romance International* had a very slow start. For a couple of years, the site had roughly twenty-five hits a day. Some days were even less. By the beginning of 2007, the photo gallery was getting approximately 125 visitors a day. To date, the gallery has gotten over 71,500 visitors. This did not happen in a year or even two years. This may not seem like much, but when you are operating on half a shoestring budget, to me this is pretty darn good!

In late February 2007, the network powering *One World Singles* sent out a general e-mail to all its affiliate members warning it was removing sites that were inactive, and sites that did not point to their servers. Of course, I did not think this applied to my site. In my coherent mind, my site was active; it was definitely pointing to their servers and was bringing in new members.

Unfortunately, they felt 456 members were not active enough. In late March, they removed my site and closed my account, because in their words, *My site was inactive.* I said, *Inactive, how could this be?* After all, people were joining. My lowest month was February 2007 with eight members. Then in March, membership picked up. By March 21, 2007, twenty-two people became members, and more were sure to join. I understand not everyone visiting my site will join, and not everyone who joins will upgrade to become a paid member. To me it takes time to put together a large membership database.

I asked the network, "Why did you remove my site?" Their response was, "We are tightening up and working to offer a leaner, meaner Partner program which functions more efficiently and maintains our high brand quality across the Internet."

After reading that paragraph, I finally got it. Nowadays, instant gratification seems to be the norm. You see it all around you. Everything is hurry, quick, and flash! The phase, *I want it all, and I want it now* appears to be the trend these days.

The belief seems to be, when you start a business, you must make the money instantly. If this does not happen, it is time to throw in the towel. We all like to think that when starting a company, we are going to make fast money in no time, but life does not work that way.

You must build trust before you can get loyal customers, and be around for a while before people will spend their hard earn money on your product or service. When it comes to running a dating site, creating a trusting and lasting relationship with your members is more important than quick profits.

While searching the Internet for another dating network, I came across an affiliate program and read some of their testimonials. This particular testament struck a chord with me; it was honest and to the point. I am paraphrasing what the person wrote:

*I joined an affiliate almost 4 years ago now, and was informed that it would probably take around 4 years before I started to earn a reasonable income as an affiliate. I now have over 1,500 members registered and with the new site design, this promise is coming true. Affiliate payments have become easy to request and are paid on time as requested. Anonymous*

This acknowledgment summarizes the point I have been trying to make. If you are thinking about starting an online dating business or any type of establishment, remember it is not a get rich quick scheme; it is a long-term commitment where earnings may be a long time coming.

Everyday you read about companies becoming successful overnight. However, this is the exception and not the rule. You have to ask, "How long did it take the business to succeed; what mistakes were made along the way and were there any failures before the successes?"

As a professor once said in a *How to Start a Small Business* class, which I took in college, "Owning a business is 90% perspiration and 10% aspiration."

*Chapter Two*

## What Happened Next?

You are probably wondering if I found a network to power and host *One World Singles*. The answer is yes. It did not take long to find this service. After much research, I decided to take the plunge and signed on, for better or for worse. This company offered great tools and features. There were templates to design my own site. A newsletter suite to contact my members and an online directory to build my very own link exchange were also included. The site offered an affiliate program so other webmasters could promote my dating site and make money, and optimization tools to help my site rank higher in search engines.

It took about a week to get my site up and running. Since I already had a domain name, I did not have to worry about exploring a new one and registering it.

In order for my site to point to the new network, I had to create a CNAME record to point to the URL (Uniform Resource Locator is the unique address for a file that is accessible on the Internet) hosting my dating site. This was confusing. I did not have the foggiest notion as to what this all meant.

CNAME pronounced (se-nam) is short for canonical name, also referred to as a CNAME record. It is a record in a DNS (Domain Name System) database. It indicates the true or canonical host name of a computer with whom aliases are associated.

In order to be connected, a computer hosting a Web site must have an IP (Internet Protocol) address to the World Wide Web. The DNS resolves the computer's domain name to its IP address, but sometimes more than one domain name occupies the same IP address. This is where the CNAME is useful. A machine can have an unlimited number of CNAME aliases, but a separate CNAME record must be in the database for each alias. I tried doing it myself, but it was fruitless.

Before I found the new network, I had my web site address forwarded to my blog that explained why my dating site was down, temporarily. When I created a CNAME record, there was a conflict. Therefore, my web address never pointed to the server that was hosting my dating site.

I was still baffled. Finally, I decided to ask the service where I registered my domain name for assistance, and they took care of everything. I mention this, because if you choose to start a dating site, you may have to perform this task. However, do not worry; the company where you register a domain name should be able to assist you.

On April 6, 2007, my new site went live. I knew it would not be easy, because I lost my 456 members due to the closing of my previous account. However, I was determined to put in a lot of blood, sweat and laughs to make this site work.

I submitted a paid listing on several popular dating directories, and on an online dating magazine. In addition to paid advertising, I always take advantage of free advertising. Some of my best responses have come from free classifieds and free promotional sites.

Right from the start, I was getting over 100 hits a day; people were joining as regular and paying members. Five people became premium members during this month.

During the month of May, upgrades nearly tripled. This was a surprise to me. I never received upgrades so quickly in such a short period. I was happy as a bee making honey.

June started out slow. I was starting to wonder if the party was over, because the previous two months started out with a bang. So why was I in a panic mode? Sometimes I worry when people do not join at once. You would think by now I would be accustomed to the highs and lows of running an online dating site; but you can never become too comfortable. You always have to be on your toes, even if you are not a ballet dancer.

It is a couple of days into June, and no one has joined. Of course, June is a very busy month. People are planning for Father's Day, graduations, weddings, vacations, and other festive events; but when did these celebrations ever stop anyone from searching for love. It is like saying people stop or put off having intimate times together because a particular month is so action-packed.

A few days later, several more people came aboard. Hurrah! Then I noticed the hits to my site started to increase. The site was getting close to 200 hits a day. The hits started to increase more, especially during the weekend.

Throughout the second week of June, the site was getting over 250 hits a day, and nine people became premium members. Wow! I could not believe it. I said, *From where are these hits coming?*

In the meantime, I joined my dating network's forum, introduced myself as a new member, told them about my dating site, and said I would be delighted to exchange links with any dating, romance and relationship site.

It was now the last week of June, and several more people joined the site. However, I noticed the hits had dropped to around 150. It reminded me of the stock market. During this period, the market was volatile. Was there a relationship between the vicissitudes of the market and the number of hits my site was receiving? Only time would tell.

The next day, the hits went back up to over 250. Moreover, the market did go up that day. During the last four days, the number of hits to my site remained about the same. Two more people became full members. However, just as I started to jump for joy, eleven members were terminated.

Termination can occur for the following reasons:

- Payment was not made when due.
- There was a breach of the Terms and Conditions set forth by the site.
- The person failed to provide, within a specified time, any information requested to determine the accuracy of information posted by a prospective member.
- A fraud occurred.

The site did not make any money in June, because twelve full members were terminated. Nevertheless, these types of problems do occur, and are par for the course, when running an online dating site.

Meanwhile, I was waiting for my commission payment for the months of April and May. Payments are one month in arrears; when the balance is over twenty pounds, a person would receive their commission. My balance was definitely over this amount. I received my first payment on July 4. For the first time in several years, I was able to pay myself first. Yippee!

The first week of July began quite nicely. People were joining in good numbers. Approximately three people were joining each day. I was still getting over 200 hits a day.

In the meantime, I started to put together a newsletter for my members and decided to send it out quarterly, starting with the July issue. It is a good way to remind your members that they have an account with your site, and encourage them, if they have not already, to become paying members. It inspires them to come back to the site and use it again. The features in the newsletter suite allowed me to send out specific bulletins aimed at members who had unread messages in their inbox, and to members that had not uploaded a photo to their profile. It was also an excellent approach to get feedback from members. My newsletter went something like this:

*Dear Members:*

*At One World Singles, our members are the primary focus of everything we do. We want to provide the level of service that will best meet your dating, and romantic needs, and want to take this time to thank you for becoming a member of our service.*

*If you have not done so yet, please think about upgrading your membership. In addition, do not forget to tell your single friends and associates about the benefits of becoming a member of One World Singles.*

*Besides the dating site, we have a blog called One World Singles Blog. This blog includes links to popular blogs, dating and pen pal sites, dating and relationship articles, singles' events and advice columnist Miss Know It All who will provide fun and humorous answers to your dating and romance questions. Please check it out.*

*If you have any success stories in meeting someone on One World Singles that you would like to share, we would like to hear from you. Stories submitted become the property of HMCS and may be published on our blog or in any other media without any compensation to the person submitting the story. When submitting your story, please include your name, age and the country where you reside. If we publish your story, only your name and country will appear. We have the right to edit your submission for clarity. Send your stories, comments or suggestions to our e-mail address.*

*Again, thank you and enjoy your membership at One World Singles.*
*Best regards,*
*One World Singles Team*

On July 6, one hundred forty authorized members received the announcement. Authorized members were those who had signed up through the site and had activated their accounts. I could not wait for the reactions.

People were joining my site in droves. So far, six people became full members. I was not sure if the newsletter had anything to do with this occurrence. Up to this point, I had not received any comments. Fortunately, I did not put down a large wager on getting feedback, because I would have lost big time.

I decided to search the Internet for sites to submit my affiliate program and came across several directories. My affiliate program offered a two-tiered program with a 50 percent recurring revenue share generated for the lifespan of each member with a generous two-tiered recurring commission structure of 45 percent commission on Tier 1 and 5 percent commission on Tier 2.

On July 15, I went to **Yahoo!® Answers** to get some ideas as to what people's thoughts were on joining an online dating site. You can ask questions on any topic and get answers from bona fide people. My question was, "Have you ever joined an online dating service?" Visitors had three days to submit their answers. Well, I received six responses that same day:

1. *Yes. Posted by C*
2. *Yes...be very careful...it can be a breeding ground for psychos and predators... Posted by SA*
3. *Vivienne, there is nothing wrong with trying out an online dating service. Many people are trying it*

*nowadays, and it is a great way to narrow down your searches and get exactly what you want in a person. Just be cautious at first. If you need any help with dating, I would be happy to give you a free messenger consultation. I have coached many women like you to become exceptional daters and find their true love. Posted by DS*

**4.** *Nope. I do not believe in online dating services; so I have never joined. No offense to those who have joined. Just a request; be damn careful! Posted by A*

**5.** *Yep. Posted by C*

**6.** *Yes. I have actually joined several in the past. They are a good way of meeting people. Just like meeting people anywhere, you have to be cautious and make sure that person is genuine. Posted by ST*


Judging from the responses, a large number of singles have joined an online dating service. Wow!

Since I did not receive any pointers on my newsletter, I figured no response was a good response. However, on

July 17, I received a message from the dating network's forum:

*One World Singles is FILLED with fake profiles set-up by scammers. After one of their predators tried to get me, I attempted to contact One World, but NONE of the e-mail addresses listed on their site seemed to work. They got me for a subscription fee: but it could have been a lot worse. Beware: if you get scammed on this site, there is NO ONE to contact!*
*Posted by VB of Bangladesh*

My response was:

*Sorry to hear that you were contacted by a scammer. If you have any complaints, please address them to the administration department. They handle all complaints and administrative duties. It is very important to check out a person before forming any type of relationship. You said that someone tried to get you. What exactly does that mean? No one can get to you unless you give out personal information that would cause him or her to come after you.*

*Again, please accept our apologies for the inconvenience that    has resulted from this unfortunate incident.*

I forwarded the message to administration, asked them to check into this and to get back to me. The following message was on the forum the next day:

*Hi, if you do have any problems with the site, please contact us straight away with the member ID of the account you wish to report. We will remove any profiles that are brought to our attention as scam profiles. Posted by A*

Grievances like this, whether just or not, do happen. You may feel the complaint is a personal attack on you, but it is not. As far as the person is concerned, he or she is writing to a company and does not care if it is a one-person operation or a conglomerate made up of 1,000 employees.

Some people will lash out at the dating site for any personal problems they encounter with other members; it goes with the territory. It is important to remember that not everyone who joins a dating site will have good intentions. This is why the dating service must make every effort to protect or release itself from all liabilities.

A dating company may not have the capacity to investigate every person who joins his or her site. This is why an individual must take the time to investigate and get to know someone before forming any type of relationship, whether it is online or in person.

Some dating sites do have the tools to check people before they can join, but if a person is out to con someone, then he or she will find a way to do it. Nothing is 100% foolproof. It is very important to read the terms, agreements and general safety advice provided by dating sites before joining. Surprisingly, many people neglect to do this; once you have signed on with a dating site, you have agreed to their contract and may not have any recourse if you become a victim of fraud.

Most dating sites will deny any fault or liability for the consequences of a dispute or false information, which may have originated during an interaction between two people. You are solely responsible for the exchanges that you initiate with posters and respondents to the ads found on a site.

Not everyone who complains has a legitimate cause. People are always plotting and planning to separate you from your money or to get something for nothing. I have had people write to me and say, they had placed an order for my printed publication and claimed they never receive it. When I checked my database, there was no record of an order placed by these individuals. I would then write and ask them to send documentation or proof, such as a cancelled check or a money order receipt, because mistakes do happen. You probably guessed by now, I never heard from them again.

I once read of a man writing to the publisher of a magazine for singles saying that he had sent two dollars in cash requesting information about their service but never received the information. The publisher sent him the brochure, even though there was no record of the magazine ever receiving his order.

The man wrote a second time claiming that he never received the second order and sent another two dollars in cash but still had not received his brochure. The publisher finally realized that the man was trying to get something for nothing.

You have to ask, *Why would anyone send cash the second time if he did not get the order the first time?*

People say cash is king, and individuals take that expression literally. However, one should never send cash through the mail when ordering an item, because cash cannot be traced, unless it is part of a bank heist. How do you know if someone has sent you cash?

I have gotten letters that read, *Enclosed is two dollars; please send me information on your service.* No cash was enclosed. When I receive this type of mail, I will write back to the person and inform him or her that no cash was enclosed, or ask them to have the post office place a tracer on their letter. Of course, I would never hear from that person, because he or she knew no money was enclosed.

I have gotten cash from far away places. My brochures, flyers and ads have the following notation: *Please do not send cash or foreign currency. If you do, it is at your own risk*. Yet, people will insist on sending cash. I always make a note of the amount of money received.

Since I am the only person who handles the orders, the customer will get their product, as long as payment is enclosed.

Because companies want to maintain a good reputation and avoid being bad-mouthed by a *disgruntled* customer, many companies will go ahead and send the order, even if there is no record; they will contribute the error to bad record keeping or write it off as a bad debt. However, if you are a small business or a one-person operation trying to break even, you do not have the luxury of writing off bad debts, because someone is trying to pull the wool over your eyes.

Something else that really boggles my mind is some people will send cash and neglect or forget to put a return address on the envelope. I mention this because people have responded to an old or discontinued ad. What if the company went out of business or moved? The forwarding of that letter to the new address may have expired.

I received an order for my brochure; the person enclosed two dollars in cash but forgot to include his full name and address on the envelope and in the letter. He must have thought I was a mind reader. I held on to the letter for two years, thinking he would write and inquire about his request, but I never heard from him. Go figure!

If you are collecting money from your dating site or any type of business, it is extremely imperative to keep good records. Retain all receipts and details for at least two years or longer, if space permits. Do not rely on keeping information only on your computer. Make a backup copy and a hard copy of all proceeds received, and orders filled. If that computer crashes, all or some of your files may be lost forever.

On July 21, I decided to ask another question at **Yahoo!**® **Answers**, "Do you think there are too many dating sites on the Internet?" Again, respondents had three days to answer the question. I got one response:

*Nah...there is something for everyone...and if you don't find anyone, you need to stop surfing! Posted by FH*

The month of July ended up being a total bust. I had fourteen upgrades of which thirteen were fraudulent accounts. I asked myself, *What was going on here?* Of course, it had only been three months since I signed on to the network; at this point, I didn't know what to expect next and started to wonder if these terminations were going to be the norm rather than the exception. One positive note: the site was still getting over two hundred hits a day. I went ahead and purchased a three-month subscription for a featured ad in an online dating directory.

Since visitors were not interested in just meeting people by snail mail, on July 27, I added an adult dating and personals system to *HMCS Romance International.* Visitors would now have instant access to thousands of profiles and media from genuine adults, looking to meet others for intimate encounters, parties, and all sorts of other adult fun and services.

I still kept the photo gallery, and renamed the page *Meet by Mail*. If a visitor was interested in contacting someone in the photo gallery, he or she could purchase individual names and addresses.

After careful pondering, it was not fair to have visitors buy all the names and addresses if they were only interested in contacting one or two people.

I decided to continue printing the publication. It would only be sent by snail mail. After all, there are those who still wish to correspond by mail.

# *Chapter Three*

## Making Dollar$ and Cent$

When I decided on the title, *Making Dollar$ And Cent$ Out Of Online Dating*, I wasn't joking. My sites were literally making a fistful of dollars and a couple of cents. After all, it took two months to make a three-figure sale from *One World Singles*. Since there were no sales in June and July, I thought it could only get better. I was forecasting that sales would double during the next three months with fewer or no terminations. Was this a dream on my part? No! There is nothing wrong in thinking big, because there will be days when self-doubting will rear its ugly head.

While I was reading the newspaper on August 2, I decided, just for fun, to check my horoscope. It read, *You're very busy and you're making a very good impression. You're not making a fortune yet, but don't give up. This is how you get there.*

Well, this has been the story of my life. For over 20 years, I have been full of activity and making a good impression. As of yet, I have not made a fortune. I am still trying to get there, and I have not given up the fight. As the saying goes, *I have been there! I have done that! What is next?* Hello! I could have predicted this scenario.

August is known as *the dog days of summer*. Perhaps it is too hot to search for love, because many folks are vacationing, traveling or having fun at the beach. So why would anyone want to take time out his or her busy schedule to surf the Internet for romance? Do the seasons really influence the surfing habits of people when it comes to searching for love?

Therefore, on August 3, I went back to **Yahoo!**® **Answers** and asked, "Which season of the year are you most likely to meet someone?"

Within minutes, and before I could say jackrabbit, my e-mail box was full of answers to my question:

*1.  Doesn't matter; it's like the birth signs affecting love. Posted by N*

*2.  It doesn't matter much. Depends on what time of the year you get out most. However, personally, I think winter is the best because the holidays are near, and it is just a happy time of the year. People are always the friendliest then, I think. Posted by IWS*

*3.  I think summer because people are on vacation and out of college and out of their house; so you can meet them. Posted by CH*

*4.  It doesn't really matter. But I seem to get most of my action in autumn and winter. Posted by B*

*5.  Fall. Posted by BG*

*6.  I think the fall is the best time. Warm weather makes people want to play the field too much. Posted by A*

*7.  I don't think it matters, but I personally like fall because it's when you see the majority of people again; since over the summer, everyone is on vacation, or busy, the getting together with people in the fall gives you something to talk about and chances to meet new people. Posted by R426*

**8.** *It comes when it comes; you can't plan it. Though it seems around any major holiday, everyone is a bit more open to finding someone. Personally fall for me is the best time to meet someone new. Posted by BB*

**9.** *It doesn't matter; but I will say two of my better relationships started in late summer/early fall. Maybe that is just "my" time. I'm a fall baby; so I may just flourish more in the fall. Posted by SP*

**10.** *It doesn't matter, as long as you have someone that you like. Posted by JN*

**11.** *They say the fall/winter is the best time of the year...you can give someone your coat, or warm somebody up, or sit by a fireplace...and well, personally, it's something about the fall that I absolutely love. It is so romantic and quiet. Leaves are falling and changing colors. It is the perfect time for a romantic walk. I can't wait for the freaking fall now. Posted by J*

*12.   Winter, because it's cold outside and you can stay indoors. You can be more romantic because you could sit by the fireplace, cuddle, and drink hot cocoa together. More people spend more time in their house, and being in the house could lead to great things. Posted by AFM*

*13.   Summer, because everyone is starting to come out of hibernation to look for that summer love. Posted by AO*

Therefore, the season does not matter, but many respondents still have their favorite time of the year for finding that special someone. When you really get down to it, people will forever be looking for and finding companionship, no matter what season it is.

If I thought the month of August was going to be any better, I was sadly mistaken. During the first week, the number of hits to *One World Singles* kept going up and down, from 100 to 200 a day; five paying members were eliminated. I decided to grab the bull by the horn and inquired as to why my site was getting so many terminations.

The network replied saying, *More than likely it is because of "spammers" and fake accounts created using stolen credit cards. We have to cancel these accounts and refund the credit card.*

It appeared as though the summer months were bringing out the good, the bad and the hideous. Here you are thinking your site is making money, but before you can blink an eye, the money is gone. However, I am an optimist and a pessimist. So things will get better, or worse.

It was now mid August and no terminations. I kept my fingers and toes crossed, but before I could uncross them, there were two more terminations. So far, my site had thirty-two fraudulent transactions. *Ouch!*

I started to wonder why the network did not have the capability of detecting these many fake accounts before they had a chance to upgrade. I decided to write and ask if there was any way the system could detect scammers or credit card frauds before posting payments to its affiliates, and if other sites were having the same problems. I went to the forum to post the same query. I have seen dating sites claiming they are fraudulent free and can block deception quickly.

If a person uses a stolen credit card, and the network must provide a refund every time, the server and the dating site will soon suffer financially. Before long, the dating site will begin to lose faith in that network and start to search for another server to host his or her site.

In addition, members will start to have trust issues with my dating site. I am presently a partner with a couple of affiliates and have never had problems with charge backs. These affiliates never post earnings until the payments have been verified.

At this point, I was ready to start looking for another partner to power *One World Singles*. Perhaps I gave the network something to think about, and they were working on designing a program, which would block pending bad transactions. Then on August 27, I received the following comment from a webmaster in the forum:

*It's a good and valid query. Ongoing online dating scams are the matter of worry nowadays. Singles are facing a lot more problems due to this. In my concern, every dating site should enable the security feature for their paying members to protect them from scams or credit card frauds. If not then the member may leave the site.*

*Posted by a dating webmaster*

After reading that message, I started to wonder if members were leaving or not upgrading because of these problems.

On the last day of August, my site was getting over 100 hits. Could this be the start of something good?

September had finally arrived. However, I had no illusions that this month would be any better and started to search for another system to host *One World Singles*. It is always important to have a backup plan.

Of course, my personal computer was starting to act crazy; it would freeze up while I was on the Internet, and was slower than pouring molasses. My six-year-old PC had so many threats; not even a popular anti virus software was able to remove them all.

It was now time to face the music and upgrade my system. I bought a brand new desktop computer, printer and scanner. Since I was on a rigid budget, buying a PC with all the bells and whistles was not in the cards. Nevertheless, the PC I purchased served my purpose. I transferred most of my files from the old machine into the new one and familiarized myself with all the new applications and programs.

At first, it was a bit overwhelming, but ultimately everything fell into place. I was now ready to take the dating world by storm.

It was the second week of September. So far, there were no terminations, and people were still joining the dating site. I decided to hold off on seeking another network to host my site and wanted to see if things were going to get better. I should have known better.

Since adding the adult personal ads feature to *HMCS Romance International*, the site had received roughly seven hundred visitors.

The last week of September was here. Even though people were joining the site, none of them became paying members. I was of the opinion that it was better to have free members than to have paying members who ended up being fictitious. In this business, you can never win for losing.

October had started out quite sound. The hits to *One World Singles* had started to increase again. Mind you now, the stock market was over 14,000. *HMCS Romance International* had passed its 1100 visitors mark, and I was getting e-mails just about every other day from webmasters who were requesting link exchanges to this site. So far, there were no terminations at *One World Singles*. This time, I was keeping my eyes, arms, and legs crossed.

I finally heard from the network regarding my question back in August as to whether they had ways of detecting scammers or credit card frauds prior to posting payments to their affiliates. Their reply was as follows:

*We have a team that is constantly on the look out for spam/fake accounts. Any accounts, paying or not, that are discovered to be fake or spam are removed. Posted on October 9, 2007 by M*

Hearing from the network restored my confidence. For now, I decided not to pursue another partner for my dating site.

I put together my second newsletter, which read as follows:

*Dear Members:*

*We at One World Singles hope you are enjoying your membership, and that you are taking advantage of the many features that our service has to offer.*

*Please remember to take the utmost care when interacting with other members on our site. Never give out personal information until you are comfortable with the person you meet online. In addition, never send money to anyone who request financial assistance, no matter how well you think you know that person.*

*Please make certain that you examine the site's Terms and Conditions of Use.*

*With the holidays coming upon us, now is the time to start your hassle-free shopping for unique and humorous gifts for your friends, family and associates.*

*NaughtyTees Boutique offers a wide selection of T-shirts, caps, stickers, mugs and other items with non offensive, funny, raunchy, sexy, political and life-saving messages for people who enjoy wearing their sense of humor, spreading good humor around the house or office or giving a gift that expresses a woman's or a man's outlook on humor. Orders are shipped worldwide. For more details, go to NaughtyTees Boutique.*

*Thank you for being a part of One World Singles and happy searching for that special someone.*
*Best regards,*
*One World Singles Team*


The newsletter was sent to two hundred sixty active members on October 15, 2007.

October turned out to be an all right month. During the last week, the site was getting over 100 hits a day. There were two upgrades and no terminations. *Yippee!*

November had arrived. People are usually preparing for the imminent holidays. Whether individuals plan to search for love or shop for gifts was a toss-up. Some people have a tendency to breakup with their lovers around this time to evade buying gifts. How cost-conscious can one be?

However, I did read an article that said the holidays are not the time to search for a love interest, because many people are sad during this period.

Therefore, I went back to my old standby **Yahoo!**® **Answers** to test this theory and put forth the following question, "Is it difficult meeting someone during the holidays?"

I received the following two responses:

*1. I'm not sure, but I am looking and it's the holidays. I do not think I look lonely. It's not like I am asking every guy I see out; I am just checking them out and if the right one comes along then hey looks like I'll be having a nice Christmas. Posted on November 19, 2007 by CN*

*2. No you can meet people anytime of the year. Posted on November 19, 2007 by MM*

There are those who are lonely and may be surfing the web for companionship, and with a little bit of luck, they will find love and pleasure on my two sites, whether they are down in the dumps or not.

*One World Singles* was getting anywhere from 100 to 200 hits a day. *HMCS Romance International* had 1528 visitors.

Soon you begin to realize that the dating business is a fickle one. You can never rely on any business being consistent. There will always be peaks and valleys in the world of online dating. You can not get caught up predicting how many visitors are going to come to your site, or how much money you are going to make on any given day, week or month.

If I thought things were finally going efficiently, I had another thought coming. History was about to repeat itself for the second time.

On November 16, 1 received the following message from the network hosting *One World Singles:*

*Good Morning Vivienne:*

*I was taking a look at your account and it looks like your site has been the target of some unscrupulous people who have signed up to the dating system as members (with fraudulent credit cards) with the intention of spamming other users on the database. It is a common thing that many dating sites face.*

*In this instance, you have a white-labelled site One World Singles that seems to have been the target.*

*There have been numerous chargeback requests and fraudulent credit card transactions reported on transactions through this site. This is something that we need to rectify, as it is not beneficial to either of us. As it stands, your affiliate account shows that you owe us about twenty pounds because of all the fraudulent activity.*

*The best way to rectify this in a robust manner would be to delete this account. If you are still promoting xxxxxx through One World Singles, we can set up another site for you. I understand that this will cause some inconvenience for you, as you will probably have to update some links wherever you are promoting the site, but it is definitely in your interest.*

*We need to tackle this as soon as possible, and have scheduled your account deletion for Monday morning. If you have any comments or questions, please do not hesitate to get in touch with me.*

*Regards,*

*MD Affiliate Manager - NSI Limited*


However, on the same day, I received this e-mail:


*I have recently joined the xxxxx affiliate team and I would like to take this opportunity to introduce myself.*

*We have a number of things in the pipeline including some great new creative and a new website with improved navigation, which are bound to help conversions, plus an improved affiliate interface. There are also continuous improvements being made to the newsletters we send out to members in order to increase activity and improve conversions.*

*In the meantime, though, I would love to know what you think of the site and the program. Any comments - especially if you are encountering any problems with our systems would be much appreciated.*

*We do not seem to have a website for your account in our system. Could you please let me know the URL of the site you are using to drive affiliate traffic? If you are not currently promoting xxxxx site, we would be glad to explore what we can do to help you get up and running again.*

*To log into your affiliate account, please visit xxxxx and use the following details:*

*Username: xxxxx*

*Password: xxxxx*

*Please do not hesitate to either call me or e-mail me if you have any questions at all. Thank you.*

*MD*

*Affiliate Manager*

At this junction, I did not know what to think and sent the following note:

*Thank you for sending me information regarding your creative ways to improve the site, but it doesn't do me any good if you're going to delete my account from your network.*

I thought to myself, this did not make any sense. What good would it have done for the network to set up another site for me, as if fraudulent transactions would discontinue, because I had a new spot. Get real! Back in August, when these problems surfaced, the network should have done something then.

Moreover, what type of action has the network taken to lessen these types of frauds? Instead of coming up with creative ways to help visitors navigate the site easier, why not concentrate on developing a plan that would prevent or minimize bogus transactions?

Why say, "You did not seem to have a website for my account in your system?"

It sounded to me like management did not know which end was up. So now, I was at an impasse.

It did not take long for me to make a decision. Giving up my domain name or quitting was not an option. I was determined to keep on keeping on. I sent an e-mail to management informing them that I was leaving their network and wished them every success in their endeavors.

On November 18, I signed on with a new company, created an account and selected an affordable payment plan for prospective members. Designing my site with the new organization was uncomplicated. Their wizard tool was exceptionally helpful. I had chosen a warm pink and black theme for my site. If warranted, more pages with content could be added later.

To get my site to work with the new network, I had to point my domain name server to their hosting server, and then I had to notify the network when the change was made. In 24 hours, *One World Singles* went live, for a third time.

The new system provided many options for my dating site. I had the choice of blocking certain countries from joining my site. Members would have access to singles from around the world and could select to receive e-mail notifications when their profile got a new message or when people joined within their area. Premium members had access to an instant messenger program, which allowed them to contact other paying members directly.

The site started with 188,902 pre-existing profiles. It was now up to me to use my advertising and marketing knowledge to get people to visit and join my newly designed site. This was not going to be a simple task, because I had lost all of my members from the prior networks.

It had been a week since my new site went up, and no one had joined. In the meantime, I had to notify the webmasters who were exchanging links with my site that modifications were made and where they could find their links. Fortunately, there were only a few links.

During the last week of November, one person submitted a profile. Since the system did not provide a tool to indicate the number of visitors my site was receiving, on the last day of November, I added a web site counter to my site. The counter includes statistics, tracks the amount of traffic received, and provides information and graphs for historical data.

It was now December, and the visits to my site had dropped considerably. I could not figure out why my site was receiving hits in the hundreds from the prior network but only a minute number of hits from the current server.

*HMCS Romance International* was not doing any better. The visits remained consistent throughout the month; people were joining, but no one was becoming a premium member. At this point, I was strongly thinking about closing down this site and just concentrating on *One World Singles*. It did not make any sense to keep on promoting and advertising a site that was no longer bringing in any money.

At last, *One World Singles* had a Page Rank of three. Page Rank or PR is a numerical assessment that indicates how important a page is on the web and measures the number of links to your site as well as the quality of the sites providing the link. The higher the number, the more significant your site is.

It was the second week of December, and another visitor became a member. To try to get more visitors to my site, I purchased a hot link on a popular social networking site, a text link on an online directory and a listing on a popular love blog.

To get more traffic to my site, I joined a couple of social networking communities. At the end of the year, my site had over 400 visitors and 10 members. What a terrific way to end 2007.

# *Chapter Four*

## Out With the Old - In With the New

Two thousand seven was a volatile year, just like the stock market. The end of the year could not have come fast enough for me. With all the trials and tribulations, it was an unforgettable year. I could not believe it was almost two years ago when I started *One World Singles* and was looking forward to 2008 being a better year. After all, it is leap year and a wonderful time to find the love of one's life. I was predicting that singles would leap like crickets to my site and find romance, love or a lifetime partner.

By March, my site was bit-by-bit becoming somewhat popular. So far, I had over 1100 visitors to my site. I was getting an average of twelve visitors a day. There were a total of thirty-seven registered members and one upgrade. Sixty percent were males, and forty percent were females. I was pleased with these numbers, because my site was actually getting authentic individuals as members.

When I went to update my site, I was reading some of the comments from other dating partners in the network. One webmaster asked if it was possible for the server to place a *seal of approval* or *hacker safe* notice on all of the dating sites in their system. This would probably encourage more members to upgrade.

When I read that suggestion, it got me thinking as to why many of my members were not upgrading. People are more likely to become paying members if the site provides visitors with a sense of security.

I immediately e-mailed management and told them it was a great idea to have these symbols on the homepage, because they may also prevent or lessen fraud. I had more than my share of fake credit cards and fraudulent accounts with the prior network.

The next day, I got a reply from administration saying, they would forward my recommendation to their development team.

The end of March was here, and it was definitely a turbulent month. The number of visitors kept going up and down, just like the stock market.

It has been four months since I joined the new network. So far, the dating site has received over 1400 visitors, and a couple of dating sites have joined my link exchange program.

Things were finally back to normal. There were forty-seven members; people were joining the site at a slow pace. What more could I have asked? All the same, I will continue to put all of my efforts into *One World Singles*.

I have closed down *HMCS Romance International*. It was not an easy decision, but holding on to something that was not producing any revenue did not make good business sense. The way I see it, all good things do come to an end, and when one enterprise closes, another undertaking commences.

It is the third week of May and *One World Singles* has received over 2000 visitors and has 59 members and still 1 upgrade since its inception with the present and hopefully the last server. Slowly but surely, the site is moving in the right direction.

# *Chapter Five*

## Marketing and Advertising Solutions

Getting visitors to a dating site and encouraging people to become free and paying members can be an uphill battle. I have used several marketing and advertising solutions, which have been somewhat beneficial.

Writing articles focusing on romance, dating and relationship themes are good for getting publicity for a dating site. I now write articles and fictional short stories for several media content providers.

Speaking of articles, I received my first payment for an article I wrote, which inspired me to write this book. I was so excited, me a professional writer. Who would have guessed it? This is not to say that I was new to writing; I was not. I received $5.77. I know what you are thinking. You are probably wondering; how do you stretch $5.77? You would be taken aback as to what I can do with $5.77. I did not major in Home Economics for nothing. Whether it was $5.77, $57 or $577, I was eternally appreciative. After all, I could have received zilch.

A couple of months later, I submitted another piece and received $4.03. In October, I presented my third commentary and got $3.67. My payments were small because I opted to retain exclusive rights to my writings. This way I could submit the same articles to other publishers.

If you give the publisher, exclusive rights to your writings, you would receive a higher fee, but you could not publish your articles with any other media. However, I do receive performance points. For every visitor who reads my articles or stories, I receive credits. After receiving a certain amount of credits, I will receive money, like royalty fees. This means you must submit many writings or have a huge number of people reading your work.

In November, I decided to submit my fourth article and gave the publisher exclusive rights to the writing, and for this I received $4.51.

I now submit articles and fictional short stories on a regular basis to earn extra cash, and with this money, I can treat myself to a nice hot cup of cocoa and a slice of chocolate-layered cake.

Press releases are an additional benefit. When it comes to submitting information about your business, some online services will distribute your announcements free of charge. Of course, there are sites that will dole out your news for a nominal fee. I use both.

Starting a blog is a good marketing, and advertising strategy. Blog is short for a Web log. It is a journal or chronicle where writers post entries on just about any and every topic under the sun, with the most recent entry appearing at the top of the page.

Many blogs are interactive and allow viewers to post their own comments. Having a blog helps to build your reputation, increase visibility and attract readers who might be interested in exploring your online business or service.

A blog can be personal or commercial. Setting up a blog is easy and requires very little technical or programming skills. Some blogs are simple with just plain text. Others are so elaborate that they include images, streaming video, chat rooms, mobile messaging, ads and translation features.

Many blog-hosting services will let you set up a blog, free and provide you with templates to design your site. Some services will charge a small monthly or yearly fee, depending on the type of blog you want to develop. Some bloggers offer a subscription service; others ask for donations to help maintain their sites.

I started my blog in 2006 and named it *One World Singles Blog*. Because my first network did not have the tools for link exchange or article writing, this blog served as a gateway to my dating site. The blog includes links to other popular blogs, dating and pen pal sites, dating and relationship articles written by me and other authors, events for singles, news, and advice columnist *Miss Know*

*It All,* who brings fun and humorous answers to readers' dating, romance and relationship questions.

My blog is interactive. Readers can leave comments and include links to their web sites. It is a great way to get free publicity. I also use the blog to help others promote their writings, services and businesses by doing a blur or a review about their sites or projects.

Running a blog can be time consuming. You always have to come up with new ideas that will keep your readers coming back. I added a translation feature to my blog. Visitors can interpret any text or passage into their language of choice. Translations are available in English, German, Spanish, French, Italian and Portuguese.

To earn extra income, I ask if anyone enjoys my blog, readers can subscribe for only $5 a year. I am still waiting for subscriptions, but I am not holding my breath.

Registering your site in blog directories can help bring more traffic to your site and give you more recognition. Some directories, again for a fee, will distribute your blog to their members, Search Engines, websites and RSS directories.

RSS stands for Really Simple Syndication and is a network of web feed formats used to publish frequently updated content. You can subscribe to RSS news related to a variety of topics.

Another way I try to get traffic is to sell or offer free promotional products branded with my logo and web site addresses. My online stores offer mugs, t-shirts, caps, stickers, bags and other items. I would offer a free t-shirt with my web address screened on the back to any person who ordered my printed publication by snail mail.

The best places to start a new post on your dating site are in dating and relationship forums. Now this can be tricky, because many forums will see this as commercial advertising or spamming.

Using my pen name, *Miss Know It All*, I posted a message asking if anyone had a question on dating, and romance or needed advice on how to maintain a good relationship with his or her mate, to contact me at my e-mail address. To provide the reader with more information, I listed by blog address.

The forum's policy read, *No commercial posts allowed,* but it also inferred, *As with most places on the Internet, you may make your URL part of your "signature" by typing it under your name at the end of your posts.*

Did I read this correctly, or did I miss something here? I thought listing a business web address would be considered commercial advertising. Nevertheless, I was trying to be extra careful and did not want to come over as though I was doing an advertisement spot, yeah right!

The next day, someone in the forum wrote the following comment, *I guess Miss Know It All didn't know about the report spam button...hehehe.*

*And hehehe to you*, I said to myself and thought the remark was amusing, because I came across several posts, promoting their dating sites along with their web addresses.

One went so far as to say, *Check out my new social networking site.*

What the heck, maybe I do not know it all.

I currently look for forums that offer business opportunities, permit the promotion of a site or allow you to submit a site on a link exchange basis.

Search Engines (SE) are the helping hands for any web site. Either you can pay to have a service submit your site to the top SE such as Google, MSN and Yahoo, or you can manually submit your site. Whether a person should pay to have his or her site submitted is a personal decision.

Submitting your site to search engines yourself can be tedious. If you do it manually, it may take some time before your site shows up on the SE. You must keep track of the search engines you submit to, and when you submit your site, namely at the beginning or at the end of each month.

If you submit your site too often or too soon, some search engines may consider this spamming and reject your site permanently. The rule of thumb is to submit your site once a month. Various search engines have different times for adding a Website to their database. A few do it immediately; some take as long as six months; others do it only temporarily, and many may not list your site. Others will require you to register and set up an account with their SE before they will list your site.

Some search engines submission services, that charge, may promise to have your site listed within 48 hours.

There are services that will do the monotonous job of multi-submitting the information of a site to search engines on a monthly basis, thus increasing the chances of your site being listed.

If you have an affiliate program, promote it. Many webmasters run dating sites that are forever looking to earn extra income and add variety to their sites. They can help bring more visitors to your site, because they already have a large membership base. Many singles do join two or more dating sites.

Exchanging links with other dating sites can help your site rank higher in search engines and bring more traffic to your site. Most dating sites have a link exchange form to complete, and then you submit the completed form to their administrator.

Usually it will read, *Your site information has been received and will be reviewed shortly or within 48 hours.* Some sites will require you to add their link first before they will add your link to their site. Many will ask you to place their link on your homepage. Some sites have the ability to add your site automatically; others add it manually.

However, not every site will list your link as promised, and you may never hear from them. Many times, I have placed links on my page, but somehow those dating sites failed to place my link on their sites. Now, I will give the site up to 72 hours or sometimes longer, and if I do not see my link, I will remove their links.

$$$

# *Chapter Six*

## <u>Why Do People Join Online Dating Sites?</u>

I started to wonder why, when I was with the previous network, people were joining and becoming members so soon. What was it about the site that made people join or upgrade right on the spot? Well I know now, because the majority of the upgrades were fraudulent transactions. However, my marketing and advertising procedures did not change that much. I applied the same principles from my first site to the second and third one. Of course, there were differences as I indicated previously.

Because my domain name was over a year old, I thought it was becoming more popular in the search engines. Wait a minute. My page rank was zero at the start. Some sites were not even interested in exchanging links with my site for this reason.

Now here is the kicker. Remember I said in the beginning I had another online correspondence club, which was more adult oriented. This site has been on the World Wide Web since October 2001. It had a page rank of three. The number of visitors had dropped to roughly 12 visitors a day, sometimes more, sometimes less, and yet I would receive e-mails from webmasters who wanted to exchange links with this site.

It is hard to conjecture why people react differently to various sites. Why do some sites get more hits or visitors than other sites do? What makes a person sign on to a dating site and become a paying member on the spot? Why do some people join a dating site but never become a premium member? Moreover, why do people visit a site once and never return? If I had the answers to these questions, I would probably be a millionaire by now. However, I do not. I can only guess based on my own personal experiences.

Sometimes it can be the pricing and membership structure. My first network had a monthly membership period; the second network had a 7, 30, 90, 180 and 365-day membership period, and the fees were affordable and within everyone's budget. This was good because a person did not have to commit to a long membership period.

In addition, if someone used a credit card, his or her card would never be automatically re-billed. Once the full membership expired, he or she could revert to being a regular member and could upgrade at any time by repcating thc upgradc process. With the present system, I opted for the one, two, three, six and twelve-month membership time, and the fees are very reasonable.

The layout of the site can be another factor. The first network provided an already designed site. With the second network, I decided to make my site very straightforward. No banners or popup ads appeared on my homepage. Sometime ads, especially popup announcements can be distracting and annoying to visitors.

Is the site fast and easy to navigate? My first and second network uploaded very quickly. There were thousands of custom profile pages along with photos through which to browse. Anyone could see who was on-line, receive and reply to e-mails from other members, and if interested could chat live with members.

If members had questions regarding the site, there was a forum, which the first network did not have. There was never any pressure to become a premium member. The idea for using this site was to find people to form friendships and meaningful relationships first, and the love, romance or marriage would follow later.

The present network has the same features, but recently they eliminated the chat room.

Access to fewer countries may help or deter visitors from becoming members. With the first network, visitors had access to singles from around the world, and with the second network from the USA, UK, Canada and Australia. With the present structure, visitors have access to singles from around the world.

Niche dating sites can attract many visitors. Sites catering to every color, ethnic group, age, lifestyle, religion and to people with medical conditions are exploding on the Internet. However, I am not one to limit my site. I prefer reaching an eclectic group of singles.

Payment methods can prevent many people from joining and becoming premium members. Most dating sites only accept credit cards. Unfortunately, in certain parts of the world, many people do not own or have access to these types of instruments. In lieu of credit cards, some sites will accept checks or money orders. Some sites will only accept certain currencies.

The first network accepted US currency only. The second network accepted payments and members using US Dollars, GH Pounds, Canadian Dollars and Australian Dollars. If someone did not have a credit card, a person could send his or her payment by check or money order through the mail.

My present system accepts payments in US dollars, Euro dollars and UK pounds.

Many experts say that in order to make money on the Internet, your site must receive large volumes of visitors every day. That is all fine and good, but what is the logic behind having thousands of visitors a day if no one buys your product or service, or you end up with many charge backs. How do you define large numbers?

Some dating sites boast getting thousands to a million visitors a month. Other sites receive one thousands hits a day, while many get 25, 50, 100 or 500 visitors each day. I would rather receive 25 visitors a day with a few of them buying my services instead of receiving thousands of visitors and getting no sales.

Enticing visitors to your site is not an easy job. Whether you pay for advertising or not, there are no guarantees to the amount of visitors your site will receive. How does one with a small advertising and marketing budget compete with the major dating sites that have millions of dollars to spend? The answer is *you do not*. Unless you have disposable income, or you have a million dollar trust fund, you will probably go broke trying to keep up with the big players. In most cases, these large dating services are not using their own money; they have private investors, or they are publicly held companies.

The important point I try to remember is building a trusting and lasting relationship with my customers is more important than trying to keep up with the colossal honchos.

My main objective is to run a top notch-dating site so that visitors will keep coming back. Big is not always better. Sometimes personal attention and optimum service get lost along the way when a site becomes too large at the expense of its customers. I definitely prefer quality to quantity.

# *Chapter Seven*

## Tips on Starting Your Own Dating Site

Years ago, singles normally met through the following methods: personal ads in singles' publications, matchmaking services, dating agencies, correspondence and pen pal clubs, friends, associates and family members. Today, more people are going on the Internet to find their idyllic mate.

One would think with all the dating and romance sites on the World Wide Web, a person might ask, "Is there room for another Internet service catering to the singles' market?" Apparently, the answer is yes. New dating sites are opening up every day. When I did a Google search on the keywords dating, and online dating, the former produced over 200 million and the latter almost 100 million results.

According to the 2000 Census Bureau, 44 percent of the adult population (nearly 78 million people) in the USA is single, and 40 percent have tried online dating. There are also millions of lonely singles outside of the USA.

Based on the article *Half of Brits Regularly Use Online Dating Sites Claims Survey* posted on June 14, 2007 on *TechDigest.tv*, a study found that over half of the British population has registered on two online dating sites, while 83 percent of the people have been on a dating site at some point. A third of those who registered found long-term relationships, and a quarter of them are still going strong. Six percent got married.

*The Cruel Business of Love In China,* posted on June 19, 2007 on *Online Personals Watch*, wrote that there are more than 137 million Internet users currently in China. Around 56 million of these users are using the web in order to look for love or friendship writes *iResearch*, a leading Internet research agency.

According to the article, *260m mobile phone dating user by 2012...Mobile dating and chatrooms to take in $1bn* posted on September 17, 2007 on pcadvisor.co.uk, over a quarter of a billion people will be using mobile dating and chatroom services by 2012 says a new report from Juniper Research. Juniper also found that Japan and India are currently the largest mobile dating markets.

*Ghanaians Vs Online Dating* By Sonny Yenibey Namouz and published on EzineArticles.com on October 12, 2007, said, "Ghanaians became more and more interested in the internet when online dating hit the core of their hearts. Tens of hundreds of Ghanaians have found their dream partners online and are happily married. Some date online for fun, long term relationship and marriage purposes."

People will always be searching for friendship, romance and marriage. Others will pursue folks who share similar business, professional or social interests. Anyone can help reach these people, bring love and happiness into their lives and at the same time make some money.

My motto is, *Every single person is a potential customer, and we all know at least one single man or woman who is seeking someone special.*

Therefore, if you are contemplating on starting your own online dating business, here are some helpful guidelines:

- To get started you will need a computer, modem, Web Browser and an Internet Service Provider. You can begin right in your home. It can start out as a part-time venture and lead to a full-time profit-making service.
- You can buy a dating software program, but this can be costly and can start at $49.99 and go up to as much as $1,000.00 or more.
- If you buy a software program, you will probably have to be knowledgeable in coding and programming.
- You will need to find a hosting service that can install the software and host your dating web site.
- Since you're starting from scratch with no members, you'll have to come up with ways to get

singles to join your site, but building your database can be very time consuming and expensive.

• You will need to develop a membership payment plan, membership period, and the method of payment. This means you will have to find an e-commerce or an online payment system that will process payments, which can be monthly, quarterly, semi-annually or yearly. You will also need to have a good customer support system for questions and problems that may arise.

• You will have to set up terms and conditions of use, eligibility for membership, a contract to protect your business and its members, service guarantees, confidentiality disclosure, and privacy policies.

• You can design your own Website and include a preinstalled database of singles' profiles. To do this you will need to register a domain name and find a Web hosting service. If you buy a domain name, sometimes the company will host your site free. However, you may have to put up with banner ads on your site.

An Affiliate Program may be a good choice. An affiliate program is a partner Website that refers members to the host Website, who is operating the dating site. All you have to do is place a banner or text ad into your site. Every time someone clicks on the ad and becomes a paying member, you will receive a percentage of the membership fee. You may also earn anywhere from $1 to $2 for every person who signs up to become a member.

Some affiliates will pay 45 percent, 50 percent or 55 percent commission. With most affiliate programs, you must already have your own web site. Some affiliate programs will have a minimum payout of $25, $50 or $100.

The advantage to this type of program is that you never have to worry about collecting payments. However, you do have to worry about charge backs. This is why most affiliates will hold your money anywhere from 30 to 60 days before you receive your payment.

Be careful, and do your homework if you decide to use an affiliate. I had signed up with a major adult dating site as an affiliate partner. The minimum payout was $50. When I almost reached my $50 threshold, the affiliate did something to my account that showed I had only made roughly $2.

When I e-mailed the company and informed them of their error, I never heard from the affiliate. Moreover, this site is very popular, has over ten million members (so they say) and probably rakes in millions of dollars in revenues yearly.

My biggest mistake was not making a printout of my earnings. I learned a very hard lesson. Never rely on any affiliate to keep accurate records. Keep copies of all your earnings.

I said in the previous chapter that big is not always better. To add insult to injury, this affiliate had the audacity to send me their newsletter claiming how much money they had paid out to their partners. Of course, I blocked their e-mail address from my account. I felt so much better.

However, there is more. A similar situation happened again with another affiliate. I have been with this affiliate for several years and felt it was an honest mistake. However, this time, I was prepared. I had a printout of my commissions made during that period, which I was questioning.

I sent an e-mail with the record of my earnings and waited for an answer. Within 24 hours, I heard from management. They reassured me that the same amount of money I made during that period had shown up on their records. They explained that there was a cutoff period for showing commissions made after a certain number of months.

At the end of the month, I received my payment and ran all the way to the bank with a big smile on my face.

White Label Dating Software may be the best cost-effective solution to starting an online dating site. With this program, your site is hosted on an existing network. Many of these applications cater to the advanced web designer and the novice. In most cases, you do not need to know any complicated coding or programming to create a moneymaking dating site. Sometimes you can incorporate the software right into your existing Website. There are many advantages to this type of service:

- Usually there is no charge, unless you buy the software right out; the software is completely customizable; it comes with a full database of singles' profiles; all payment and processing are done by the host or server of the site.
- You can promote the site as a stand-alone dating site or as part of an existing site.
- If you want the site to appear as though it is yours, you will need to purchase a domain name.
- Once you have obtained the name that you want, you can point your domain name to the server or network.
- Since your site will already have a database of singles with their photos and profiles, you will not have to worry about starting from the beginning to build a large membership roster. Of course, the site is fully hosted on the company's server.
- Many hosts pay anywhere from 30-60 percent commission.
- Most White Labels support a variety of member networks. Therefore, you can create a Website for a particular niche.

• Some will allow you to set your own membership fee.

A White Label Dating Site Package may be a good choice. This type of dating software is a bit different from your free White Label Software. You can sign up for an account, but you will pay a monthly fee. The advantages to having this type of account are:

• There are no set up or commission fees. You do not share any fees or commissions you make from your site with the hosting service, and the money you make is all yours.

• You get web hosting, software and 24-hour technical support.

• Your account is set up and ready instantly.

• Your can customize your site with your own logo, graphics and text.

• You can set up your own language or multiple languages, dating service locations, genders, profile questions, time zone, payment method, subscription plans and prices, domain name, e-mail, and more.

- You can add profiles included in the account so you do not have to start from scratch, or you can choose to start with no profiles.

- You can use your own merchant account or a third party e-commerce service.

Before signing on with any affiliates or servers, check them out thoroughly. Most affiliates have a support department, which should include a telephone number, e-mail and mailing address. One way to test a service is to send them an e-mail requesting additional information on their business. If you do not receive an answer within 72 hours, do not waste your time with the company.

The service you select should provide you with up to date online stats of free and full paying members that have signed up through your site or through your affiliates. There should be a record of total earnings. How much money was paid out to you, the date the money was sent and the method of payment should be noted. Most services will hold the money anywhere from one to two months in case there are charge backs. Sometimes there is a minimum payout.

Providing marketing resources and tools, effective keywords to use when advertising your site, recommended keyword generating tools, search engine and pay per clicks (PPC) programs should also be included to help promote your dating site.

The type of plan you select will depend on your circumstances. Only you can decide how much time, effort and money you will want to put into starting and running an online dating site.

However, if you decide to start an online dating site, consider the following:

✓ You will need a good sense of humor, no matter how difficult things may get.

✓ You will need to have passion and love for the business.

✓ You will need plenty of patience and fortitude.

✓ You will have to be a jack-of-all-trades and a master of all.

✓ You will make mistakes.

✓ You will have to take on some risks.

✓ You may have to live on less.

✓ You will be working long hours with no over-time pay.

✓ You can never mix business with pleasure.

✓ The buck will always stop in front of you.

✓ Murphy's Law will always come into play. Anything that is meant to go wrong will definitely go wrong.

✓ There will be days when you will want to quit.

✓ There will be no steady paycheck or stability.

✓ There will be no paid sick leave, no paid holidays and no paid vacations.

✓ It may take many years before your business becomes profitable.

✓ You will discover talents you never thought you had.

✓ You will be running a business, even if no one else thinks you are.

✓ The people who matter the most will be your customers, who can either make or break your business.

✓ The customer is always right, even if you think he or she is wrong.

✓ There will be plenty of sleepless nights.

✓ If you are thinking about borrowing money to start your venture, think twice before going to a bank.

✓ To avoid unnecessary drama, heartaches and conflicts, avoid doing business with relatives, friends and neighbors.

# *Chapter Eight*

## Conclusion

I hope you took pleasure in reading this book as much as I enjoyed writing it. *Making Dollar$ And Cent$ Out Of Online Dating* was not intended to be a how to guide but a personal journey into the daily operations of an online dating site. However, if this book inspires you to start a dating site or any other type of online company, I hope the information will be of great value to you.

I do not know what the future holds for *One World Singles*, but I would like to end this book by sharing with you some of the accolades, comments and reviews I have received from visitors, regarding my dating sites, blog and articles. These compliments have motivated me to keep on working at making my sites eventually successful.

Enjoy, and again, thank you for purchasing the book.☺

*1. Wow! Soon your blog will become single seeking love powerhouse. Keep it up. Posted on July 27, 2007 by D*

*2. One World Singles is an online dating encyclopedia created by Vivienne Neal and is suitable for all colors, ages (18+), religions, ethnicities and lifestyles. The site itself is a little dull but that is exactly the reason why it is so easy to navigate. Everything is arranged so that it is easy to find your way around and the colour scheme is calm on the eyes (and my very high-resolution LCD monitor). Vivienne Neal is quite experienced in her field and has been bringing singles together since 1986 through printed and online publication called*

*HMCS Romance International. The content itself is very complete ranging from articles like Sensual Message by Romance to Meeting and Socializing. Every post is professionally written and includes links, e-mails details and comments. All and all this blog is perfect for those who are easily distracted by pictures and advertisements and who are simply looking for unique and easy to understand dating and relationship information. Posted on August 3, 2007 by DW*

**3.** *Nice blog. My friend reads your writing on a regular basis and talks about it quite a bit. Keep up the good work. E-mail sent on August 6, 2007 by IM*

**4.** *Thanks for creating a great site for those that want to know about online dating. I appreciated your attention and wish you great online business. E-mail sent on August 20, 2007 by AK*

**5.** *I found hmcsromance.com and I really enjoyed it. The information is great and the site is easy to navigate. E-mail sent on September 25, 2007 by MH*

**6.** *Today I visited your website and found it to be really informative. I am highly pleased to see the* *comprehensive resources being offered by your site. It is indeed very informative. Kudos to you for the Great Work! E-mail sent on October 12, 2007 by S*

**7.** *Thank you for sending me your publication and T-shirt. I read from your letter that you wrote to me that you want to stop publishing or printing the publication; please, I am very sorry for that and wish to advise you to continue publishing or printing the publication because some of us prefer the publication more than the Internet. Thanks. Yours faithfully. Letter received on October 20, 2007 from SB*

**8.** *I enjoyed your content very much. Keep up the good work. Message sent on October 24, 2007 by AS*

**9.** *After reviewing your blog I think it could be a good match for the "Outsourced" film campaign that I am working on. E-mail sent on December 11, 2007 by MS*

**10.** *Hello. This post is likeable, and your blog is very interesting. Congratulations :-). E-mail sent on January 9, 2008 by CN*

**11.** *Wow very impressive. Posted on January 14, 2008 by B98*

*12.* *Found your blog interesting. E-mail sent on January 31, 2008 by M*

*13.* *Glad you enjoyed my blog! I went over to browse yours and enjoyed it immensely. You've got many talents, I gather. E-mail sent on February 11, 2008 by LS*

*14.* *Great blog. Posted on February 16, 2008 by J*

*15.* *Excellent dating site! Posted on February 19, 2008 by SD*

*16.* *Great blog! I learned something new. Posted on February 26, 2008 by A*

*17.* *Thanks for the warm welcome! I always enjoy my visits to One World Singles! Posted on March 9, 2008 by CE*

*18.* *What was that I just saw? Was it...Cupid? Some sort of "love goddess"? Think again; it's none other than Vivienne Neal – founder of One World Singles! In a sense however, I guess you could call her a love goddess of sorts. Her site is dedicated to giving you tips, advice, and answers to your dating questions and concerns! For many men and women, it can be rough taking the first steps into dating again. One*

*World Singles will help walk you through getting your feet wet again! Singles of all races, religion, and lifestyles should take the time to check it out! Posted on March 14, 2008 by AC*

19.  *I have explored your site and found it interesting. It looks professional and offers exceptional information/ products. I noticed that you have linked to other sites and thought my website can also be a part of your prestigious website. E-mailed sent on March 27, 2008 by AG*

20.  *I am a huge fan of alternative healing, am in school to become a Homeopath, and am already a Bach Flower Practitioner; so I applaud your post! You are very right and very smart!!! Posted on March 31, 2008 by L*

21.  *We loved this blog and its honest outlook and advice; that it quickly became one of our favorites. Posted on April 4, 2008 by AWP*

# *Epilogue*

It is now 2017. So much has happened since I wrote this book. When you read *About The Author,* you will see.

After weighing in on our options when it comes to the services and products we provide, we have decided to close our **One World Singles Online Dating** site. It was a great ride but with all of the dating sites online, it is hard to compete with thousands of sites attempting to reach the singles' market. We have been bringing singles together since 1986, which started out as a mail order introduction service and morphed into a worldwide online dating service.

We are now going to concentrate on maintaining our **One World Singles Blog**, selling our books and T-shirts. If you are not familiar with our Blog, check it out at http://www.oneworldsinglesblog.net. Our Blog is updated every Monday. As of December 31, 2017, the site received over 202,000 visits from around the world.

Never in my wildest dreams did I ever think I would write five more books and two stand-alone short stories. Being an author has been educational, enlightening and challenging. When it comes to writing fictional short stories, I have made every mistake you can think of and will probably continue to make more, but because of these mistakes, I feel that I will continue to become a better writer.

Nevertheless, the journey has been great. I have met so many wonderful people who have been supportive, and I hope more great men and women will come my way.

Stay well, and if you are seeking someone special, I am always here to help.

# About The Author

Born in 1946, Vivienne Diane Neal is a storyteller with a wicked sense of humor. Vivienne has been writing articles for over thirty years and started writing fictional short stories in 2007. She gets her story ideas from observing people, places and things and watching true TV court cases and talk shows.

In 2009, she wrote *Shades of Deception*, a collection of ten fictional short stories centering on diverse men and women, who in their speedy search for love, romance and bliss, become the targets and victims of deceit, betrayal, fraud, revenge and scandal.

In 2011, she penned, *Malicious Acts*, a collection of five short stories, focusing on people who will stop at nothing to get what they want. If it means disguising themselves as benevolent individuals and destroying lives along the way, they are up for the thrill. They will use romance, sex, lust, greed, manipulation, and deceit as preludes to suck unsuspecting men and women out of their life's savings.

*The Man with the White Handkerchief* is a digital short story (under 600 words) which partook in the *Lulu Short Story Contest* in 2011. The narrative is about a woman approached by a stranger who asks for directions to a specific street, but she has no recollection as to what took place after that encounter.

*Wicked Intent* is a fictional short story about a successful businessperson, who is planning to marry his self-centered fiancée, but a beautiful stranger diverts him. She will bring lust, desire and eroticism into his life but will ultimately destroy his relationship with the one person who has always stood by him.

Her fifth book, *Retribution Unleashed*, is the sequel to **Wicked Intent** and ranked No. 66 on UBAWA's (Urban Books, Authors, and Writers of America) top 100 Books of 2013. After spending two years at a sanctuary, Honeydew's mental state begins to improve. With the help of another patient, whom she despises, Honeydew will unleash her style of retribution by putting together a diabolical plan that will devastate her son and the woman she holds responsible for stealing her vast nest egg.

**Café Mocha** is an erotic romance short story about a woman who decides to change her way of thinking when it comes to meeting men.

**Deception in Plain Sight** is the author's first novel about a woman of means, who falls for a handsome, charming and cunning man. He will not only awaken her sexual inhibitions and manipulate her into marrying him, but he will also put into motion the destruction of her parents' billion-dollar empire that has been in the family for over four generations.

Now, semi-retired, Vivienne continues to write articles on love, romance, relationships and other topics of interest on her blog at https://www.oneworldsinglesblog.net

For more information, send an email to
info@oneworldsinglesblog.net

## *Sites to Visit*:

https://www.oneworldsinglesblog.net

http://lulu.com/spotlight/hmcs1946

http://www.amazon.com/-/e/B003ONO6G4

http://www.amazon.co.uk/-/e/B003ONO6G4

http://www.smashwords.com/profile/view/hmcs

www.ingramcontent.com/pod-product-compliance
Lightning Source LLC
Chambersburg PA
CDIIW051636050426
42443CB00024B/223